W9-BJE-004

To Rita

Best wishes

Kara Wilson
April 2005
New York

DECO DIVA

A one woman show
By
KARA WILSON

DECO DIVA

A one woman show
By
KARA WILSON

First Published 2005
ISBN 0 9549927 0 9

Published by
KW Publishing
www.karawilson.co.uk

Design:
Dalia Hartman
Publishing Consultant:
Richard Leonard
Printed in Oxfordshire by
David Shayler

Cover image:
Kara Wilson's study of 'The Dream'
by Tamara De Lempicka

DECO
DIVA

INTRODUCTION

The paintings of Tamara de Lempicka (1898-1980) delighted and intrigued me from first sight. How exciting to discover the woman's character was as wild and wonderful as her work. She was truly an original. A delight for any actress to portray.

In 1996 while exhibiting at the new Leith Gallery in Edinburgh, I painted portraits live in the gallery as a daily attraction for visitors. It was then I found that, unlike most artists, I positively thrived when people were watching. In other words as a painter I was more of an actress.

Thus it was that one year later when Jan Morrison invited me to come up with another event for the gallery at Festival time, I devised the idea of a play with paint – a one woman show about an artist during which I would complete an oil painting. I chose the Scottish painter Bessie MacNicol for my first subject and wrote GLASGOW GIRL.

I was able to mix narrative with songs of the period and paint my way through one of her portraits all the while. At the end of the show I had the bonus of being able to offer the painting for sale to the audience.

The genre was a hit and I seized on Tamara for the next painter to inhabit. Although comparatively little has been written about her, the idiosyncracies I uncovered were rich. The music and personalities of Paris in the thirties created a wonderful setting and the paintings were oh so seductive. It was hard to choose which painting to feature in this next show, DECO DIVA.

But when I was in New York with GLASGOW GIRL at Phillips
Auction House during Scotfest in 1999, Alasdair Nichol arranged
for me to see a privately owned Lempicka at the house of Toni
Schulman. I fell in love with the woman in the picture. It was
Rafaela, Tamara's favourite model, and my choice was made.

I used to worry that Tamara would be angry with me even at-
tempting to paint like her and tell her stories. She was a strong
woman and, I am sure, easy to annoy. But I hope she would be
more flattered by this tribute than angry at my presumption. I
have certainly loved bringing her to life on stage and my life is the
richer for her.

Kara Wilson

*Kara Wilson was born and educated in Glasgow and now lives in London
with her husband, actor / writer Tom Conti. When not acting, singing or
painting, she is to be found playing with her grandson Arthur.*

The scene is a corner of Tamara de Lempicka's Paris studio in 1939. Tamara enters, a strikingly beautiful woman in her forties. She catches sight of the audience.

Oh. You're still here. You waited.

Tamara turns and shouts offstage to her maid Clothilde.

Clothilde, I told you to get rid of them.

She turns back to the audience with disdain.

You waited. You really should not have waited.

She takes off her wrap and hat.

I was detained. I can't do the interview now. It's too late. I have to paint... for my sanity.

Clothilde, where did you put my coat?

She finds it behind the easel.

I've found it.........I've found it.... Stop looking for it..... Not that she is......

It's just not a good time. We're leaving at the week-end. This will be my last opportunity to paint - for a few hours this evening - I am going out to dinner shortly and afterwards they are throwing a party in our honour. I am afraid we must cancel the interview.

You're not leaving. All right stay. And I will talk but please do not bother me with questions. We can do this interview but on these terms. I will talk while I paint and you can make of it what you will. OK?

She turns to her easel and chooses a canvas.

I will try to forget that you are there.

She picks up her brushes and starts to paint.

I need peace. I need to paint. I can always lose myself in my work. No matter what is happening all around I can just disappear into my work.

This is Rafaela. My beautiful Rafaela.

I discovered this beauty, you know.

One day I was walking in the Bois de Boulogne and this woman was walking a little distance in front of me. Everybody who approached her, stopped and stared and looked at her. I had to see why. So I walked more quickly and when I had passed her I turned and saw why. She was indeed the most beautiful woman I had ever seen. Her eyes were amazing, her skin, her mouth........ I didn't stop to think. I spoke to her. I said "Mademoiselle, I am a painter. I would like you to pose for me. Would you do this?" She said "Yes, why not?"

I took her immediately to my car and we went home to my studio. I gave her lunch and then asked her to undress and lie down while I paint her. She undressed without shame and lay down. Every position she took was pure art - perfection. I fell in love with her beauty. I painted her for over a year.

But then the young man in the building opposite stole her away from me. He had been watching her through the window, watching her pose for me. In the end he married her and took her away.

She was a strange, sad creature. She confessed to me once that she could not live without a man. Some nights, if she was alone, she would go mad and wander out into the streets looking for a man, any man. She did not do it for money. She just craved a different man all the time. I often wonder where she is now and if this craving is still here.

I often find my models like this. One night at the theatre I saw a lady in front of me. I fell in love with her shoulders. She turned her head and her profile was perfect. It was just the face I wanted for a huge picture I was doing of five women.

I was with two young gentlemen and I warned them I was about to proposition this lady. They tried to stop me, said she was a lady and would never sit for me - certainly not in the nude which is what I would be sure to demand.

I proved them wrong. I went up to her. I said " Madame. My name is Tamara de Lempicka. I am a painter. I am working on a piece in which there are five personalities. But one face has been missing ….until now. Yours is that face. Would you sit for me".… and my heart was beating …. "in the nude?"

She came every day for three weeks. We never talked.
When it was finished, I tried to give her something to
thank her.

I said "Could I give you perfume?"
"No," she said, "I don't never wear perfume."
"Flowers?"
"No, I think flowers should remain in the garden."
"Chocolate?"
"No."
"Money?"
"No, thank you."
"Then why did you sit for me all that time?" I asked
her.
"I knew and admired your paintings. Goodbye."

And she was gone! I never even knew her name.
She knew and admired my paintings.

That's how it is. I see someone and I know there and
then that is what I am looking for. Once I was painting
a model, a girl who was posing nude - in a standing
position. She got hungry and reached for an apple from
a fruit bowl. She held the apple near her shoulder for a
moment and suddenly I saw it. She became Eve. I knew
then I had to find Adam - immediately.

I was like a crazy woman. I rushed out into the street
on my search - peering into everyone's face – looking
for my Adam and then I found him.

He was a young gendarme directing traffic - very handsome, very big, strong. I went straight up to him in the middle of the road and asked him if he would pose. Right away he said "Of course, Madame. I am an artist myself. When would you like me to come?"

He came to my studio after his work. He said "How would you like me to pose?" I answered "In the nude." He took off his clothes and folded them carefully, then piled them neatly on a chair with right on top - his re-volver.

I brought in Eve and I introduced Adam to Eve. And they posed holding onto each other in a standing embrace. I think they enjoyed it. He certainly seemed to.

I need music. I can't talk non-stop. You can stay but let's have some music.

Clothilde! Clothilde!..... Give us music...... Put on a record.... Something restful but ....inspiring.

We'll see what she makes of that!

The opening strains of Chopin's ZYCZENIE fill the room.

Oh my god. Chopin. Does she want to drown me with nostalgia?

Tamara sings along with the record in Polish as she paints.

Gdybym ja była słoneczkiem na niebie,
Nie świeciłabym jak tylko dla ciebie.
Ani na wody, ani na lasy,
Ale po wszystkie czasy
Pod twym okienkiem
I tylko dla ciebie
Gdybym wsłoneczko
Mogla zmienić siebie

This is one of the first songs I ever learnt.

Gdybym ja była ptaszkiem ztego gaju
Nie śpiewałabym wżadnym obcym kraju
Ani na wody, ani na lasy,
Ale po wszystkie czasy
Pod twym okienkiem
I tylko dla ciebie.
Czemuż nie moge
Wptaszka zmienić siebie!

(As the music fades) I used to play Chopin on the piano.

I persuaded my mother to buy me a piano - for my bedroom - I practised long and hard – until one day I realised that I would only ever be repeating what some-one else had already done. That day I closed the lid forever.

I couldn't get out of Poland fast enough. One day I was visiting a sick friend and heard the doctor saying to her mother "You must take her to the south of France to recover." That night I came home with a very bad cough - very bad indeed. It was not hard to persuade my grandmother to take me away. She loved to travel and particularly she loved to gamble - in Monte Carlo. She found my health a good excuse for a visit to the casinos but she took me to Italy as well.

We went to every gallery in Florence and Venice and Rome. It was my first experience of real art. I was about thirteen. I had not had the opportunity until then of seeing any painting that inspired me. This was so much better than school.

I had been painted. When I was young, mother commissioned a portrait of me. I hated it. I was 'une petite grosse'. This woman arrived with pastels. She was famous. I had to sit still - for hours it seemed - it was a torture. I have had my revenge since! - ah how many models have I tortured in return.

Anyway, the final picture was dreadful. It didn't look like me one bit. And the lines were not clean.

I felt sure I could do better although I knew nothing about the technique. I got some paints and persuaded my sister Adrienne who is two years younger than me to sit. I worked and worked until I had a result. It was not perfect but, to me, it was much more like my sister than the pastel was like me.

But in Italy I saw paintings I really admired. I still like to go to Italy to the same galleries to inspire myself. And I love Italians.

I was sent like all girls of my class in Poland away - thankfully - to boarding school - to Lausanne. When my mother decided to marry again, I had no interest in returning to Warsaw, so I invited myself to stay with my Aunt Stefa in St Petersburg.

That was heaven. Aunt Stefa had married a rich banker with financial houses in France and Switzerland and Austria. They lived in such luxury. They had two sons, one had a French governess, one had an English governess. The boys spoilt me. I could do anything I wanted.

Aunt Stefa had wonderful jewels. She had one drawer for diamonds, one for rubies, one for emeralds. Sometimes she would let me look through those precious drawers and choose what she would wear that evening.

Ah that was living. I knew even then I was determined to make my life as rich as hers.

Yes, life in Russia for me was very happy for the moment. Clothilde. Play us some something Russian........

But all was soon to be destroyed. The working classes went on strike and when the Tsar threw some socialists in jail, there were massive demonstrations in the street. But then war was declared between Russia and Germany and suddenly everyone was down on their knees declaring their patriotic allegiance to the Tsar on the steps of the Winter Palace and St. Petersburg became Petrograd over night.

I diverted myself from all this chaos by falling in love. I met him first at the opera. He was with two gorgeous looking women. He was a lawyer and a man about town - very beautiful. I was fifteen then and I had to make him notice me. So I walked over to him in the theatre bar and dropped a low curtsy before him. He laughed at my childish forwardness but he did notice me.

One year later my aunt and uncle threw a costume ball and they invited him to it. I knew I must be bold to attract his attention with all the glamorous and overdressed guests that would be present. So I decided on a piece of theatre. I dressed as a Polish peasant .... wait .... I was a goose girl with a basket over one arm and leading by a ribbon dangling from the other - a real live goose. You can imagine the commotion that a goose caused in the ballroom - cackling and slipping across the floor. Every head turned and I won a round of applause for my entrance and Tadeusz Lempicki, for that was his name, could not fail to notice me.

I decided he was the one I wanted.

My uncle was not so keen. Although Tadeusz was a lawyer, he didn't seem to work and had no money of his own. But when the Germans invaded Poland in 1915, we realised I would never return. I had become my uncle's responsibility and he asked me what I wanted to do with my life. I said .... I would marry Tadeusz Lempicki - no other man in Petrograd would do. So rather unwillingly he called upon Lempicki and offered him a dowry for me and arranged the marriage. I was married in the Knights of Malta Chapel with a train that stretched the whole length of the aisle.

The balalaika introduction of URALSKAYA (Music by Rodiguin, Words by Pilipenko) is heard.

Ah. Timing! ..... Russia. Ah, Russia.

Tamara stops painting and sings the song in Russian.

Вечер тихой песнею над рекой плывєт.
Дальними зарницамн светнтся завод.
Где-то поезд катится точкамн огня,
Где-то под ряσинушкой парни ждут меня.

Ой, ряσина кудрявая,
Белые цветы,
Ой, ряσина, ряσинушка,
Что взгрустнула ты?

It was only a few months before the revolution turned our world upside down. We were living in an apartment in town bought with my dowry, Tadeu had no work of course and had got somehow involved with a counter-revolutionary movement. They came in the dead of night - those long faced men in black leather - and arrested him. We were making love when they battered on the door. They threw him in prison but I could not find out where.

Everyone was leaving and seeking safety in Finland and Sweden. My mother and my sister had escaped Poland - but not my brother or my mother's new husband. They never got out. Aunt Stefa and her family managed to join them in Copenhagen. I stayed behind searching in vain for my husband. It was one of the coldest winters and I wandered the streets from jail to jail. I came across a dying horse, lying starving in the frozen slush, and I thought - that is Russia - a starving horse, dying in the street.

Finally I enlisted the help of the Swedish consul. I found him at a dinner he was giving. We talked. He said he thought he would be able to find out which jail they had taken Tadeusz to. He offered me some dinner. I refused. He insisted I sit and eat. The food was so rich. He liked me and seemed prepared to do anything for me provided I would like him in return. It seemed a small price to pay. Later in the cold night air I vomited that rich dinner into the gutter.

He persuaded me to leave with him for Finland, as a member of his entourage, with a false passport, speaking only French - no Russian, no Polish. I will not forget that train journey. I sat there rigid with fear gazing out at the frozen Russian countryside that I would never see again. At the border the Red Army guards got on the train. My hand trembled as I held out the false passport and I stumbled on the walk across the wooden footbridge into Finland. But I escaped. At Helsinki I said goodbye to the Swedish consul and left to join my family and, true to his word, he secured Tadeusz's freedom a few weeks later.

Tadeusz was morose though and did not celebrate with the rest of us our miraculous escape. We did not feel our exile would be permanent. There had been such chaos - so much upheaval - we all thought the present regime would not last long. But then the Tsar and his family were assassinated and we knew there was no going back...so we all came to Paris.

My beautiful Paris… where I have been so happy…..
and where I learned to paint … it was my sister Adrienne's idea. She studied architecture at the Ecole des
Beaux Arts as soon as she and mother settled in Paris.

I was miserable at first. We had no money. I had to sell
the jewellery I'd brought from Poland. Tadeusz had no
work. My uncle soon had a banking job to offer him
but he was too proud to take it. We started to quarrel.
He sat reading detective novels in our nasty little hotel
room. I got pregnant and then Kizette arrived. What a
struggle it was. I had to find something for myself.
Then Adrienne suggested I take up painting and my life
changed. I found a way to be successful, make
money… be my own master.

I went to the Academie de la Grande Chaumière where
the classes were free and models were provided. I went
to every session - morning, afternoon and evening.

Then I would come home and go on painting into the night. I was obsessed and determined. I started with still lives. Once I was painting a plate of little cakes, whipped cream and chocolate, but I got hungry half way through and ate one.. then another.. and another…that picture was never finished. Then I went on to portraits. I painted Kizette a lot because she was there.

I searched out the best teachers. I asked everybody. I chose Maurice Denis first. He taught me that before a painting was anything- a nude, an animal, an automobile - it was first a flat surface. And that I, as the artist, had a right to deform it - for the purpose of creating an 'emotional caricature' - all in the name of beauty. He said "Decorative painting was true painting" and style was all important.

He would not let us start drawing from life until we had achieved great skill in draughtsmanship in our still lives. He made us copy the old masters. He insisted on a simple approach which suited me well. Even as a school girl in Switzerland I did not like the messiness of the Impressionists. Cezanne's apples to me were badly drawn, not precise. But I had seen Italian 15th century apples that were so clean, so defined, so simple - not muddy and blotchy.

Next I studied with Andre L'hôte. His style mixed the decorative with the avant-garde and he distorted his nudes into mathematical shapes - a kind of geometric disintegration. He called it a 'new cubism'. He taught me to love Ingres - so you can imagine how thrilled I was later that my work was described as a kind of 'perverse Ingrism'. Wonderful. He said "La fin de l'art est le plaisir."

And then of course Art Deco was born with the Exposition Internationale des Arts Decoratifs in 1925. This mixed traditional subjects with modern techniques and concentrated on the surface of things. Full of contrasts and textures - the soft warm flesh of a nude and the cool shiny metal of the automobile. I found myself - how you say - 'in the right time at the right place'. I could learn and make use of all I learnt but I did not want to copy. I wanted to find my own style.

I believe education is like packing a trunk for a holiday. You have to take just the right amount to live in style and comfort, but know what to leave out - You do not want to make your bag so heavy you can't lift it – and – you must leave space for what you may pick up along the way.

After only a few months I had several paintings that I felt were good enough to show. Adrienne got her professor from Beaux Arts to look at them and he thought they would sell. I vowed I would buy a bracelet each time I sell a painting and very soon would have jewels all the way up to my elbow.

I took them first to Colette Weill. She asked who had

painted them. I said I did. She kept them and said she would get in touch with me. Days passed but then she asked me round. When I arrived at the gallery, a young couple came in to buy a painting. Ignoring me, Colette showed them paintings by many of her artists and included mine in the selection. After half an hour the couple left with two paintings by a young unknown artist, Tamara Lempicki. She offered me 10% and I was delighted.

Life for us started to improve. We moved to an apartment on the left bank, I bought a little yellow car, a Renault; we hired the English nanny for Kizette ... even Tadeusz was forced into taking the job at the bank. The bracelets started to mount up my arm.

Once someone from the bank came around to investigate why suddenly there was money in our account ... in an account that had been so empty before....they couldn't understand it. I asked him in to see the reason - shortly afterwards he left having bought one of my paintings for 50,000 francs.

But my success did not make Tadeusz happy. My passion for painting irritated him. I was always immersed. When I wasn't painting I was out seeing friends - sitting talking in the cafes of Montparnasse - getting excited ... about everything .. about art. One night we were at La Coupole and Marinetti was going on about Futurism and how we as artists were enslaved by the past. In a fit of passion he stood up on the table and said "Until we destroy the past, there will be no modern art. We must destroy the past. Burn the Louvre."

Very soon he had us all chanting "Burn the Louvre." I leapt up and said to him "Come I will drive you there in my car. It's just outside." We rushed out of the cafe in excitement to find that my car had been towed away by the police. So that rather put an end to our little bit of terrorism and we spent the rest of the evening at the police station.

I liked that little yellow car. I was driving it in the south of France one day, all dressed in yellow to match it. I stopped to go into Chanel. When I came out there was a note on my windscreen "You look so wonderful in your car. I would like to meet you" with a lady's name signed at the bottom and the address of the Hotel Ruhl in Nice.

Later I was in Nice and went to the hotel, gave the hall porter my card and wrote on it "This is about the car". She turned out to be the fashion director for the German magazine "Die Dame" and realising who I was, asked me to do a painting of myself in my little yellow car for the cover of her magazine. I said yes, because I knew I would be paid twice - once for the cover and once when I sell the painting. *(indicating the self portrait on the wall)* Yes, that's it…. I know it's not yellow. It's not sold either. And it's not a Renault but I thought green in a Bugatti is much more stylish, don't you think.

I like to dress to suit the occasion. I love hats. I have bought dozens and dozens. Very soon I could afford to be dressed by the best couturiers in town. They were my friends - Coco Chanel, Paul Poiret. I have such a circle of friends here. Such talent - so many painters - Van Dongen, Picasso, Laurencin, Pascin, Leger, Kisling, Cocteau, Modigliani to name a few - musicians, writers, singers, poets, philosophers - well we were all philosophers. None of them ordinary - all very bright and smart - dazzling. Ah, how we would party….The night-clubs….

Clothilde …. play Suzy's song. Suzy is my friend. Suzy Solidor. She has her own night club, La Vie Parisienne. She is becoming very famous for this song.

(As the introduction plays) Yes, this one.

Sur cette terr', ma seul' joie, mon seul bonheur
C'est mon homme,
J'ai donné tout c'que j'ai,
mon amour et tout mon cœur
A mon home
Et même la nuit, quand je rêve, c'est de lui.
De mon home.
Ce n'est pas qu'il est beau, qu'il est riche ni costaud
Mais je l'aime

C'est idiot l'm'fout des coups
L'm'prend mes sous
Je suis à bout mais malgré tout
Que voulez vous

Je l'ai tellement dans la peau
Qu'j'en d'viens marteau
Dès qu'il s'approch' c'est fini
Je suis à lui
Quand ses yeux sur moi se pos'nt
Ça m'rend tout chose.
Je l'ai tellement dans la peau
Qu'au moindre mot
L'm'f'rait fair'n'importe quoi
J'tuerais ma foi
J'sens qy'il me rendrait infâme
Mais je n'suis qu'un'femme
Et j'l'ai tell'ment dans la peau.

La Vie Parisienne, Suzy's night club, is a lesbian club - so strange she should make her name with a song called Mon Homme. I painted Suzy. It was the thirtieth portrait she had done - she has the reputation of being the most painted woman in Paris. Her portraits line the walls of her club. Ah what times we women would have in that club.

Don't get me wrong. I like men as well. I like nothing better than to paint all day and then go out in the evening with a young man who admires me all night, touches me and tells me how beautiful and talented I am. Wouldn't you?

But my choice of recreation did not go down so well with my husband. But I am an artist. I live on the fringe of society and the rules of normal society do not apply on the fringe.

He was always angry with me and I with him. He was always depressed and there was such gaiety and excitement to be had. I would dine with dukes and duchesses, princes and princesses .. my friends Prince Felix Ioussoupov and Princess Irina Alexandrovna throw such parties for all the Russian émigrés in Paris. Every Saturday –a soirée - so theatrical.

I used to come home and wake Kizette up in the night and tell her of all the grand people I had just rubbed shoulders with.

And I would take trips to Italy for inspiration every now and then. In Milan I went to see the Gallery, the Bottega di Poesia, owned by Count Emmanuele Castelbarco. I arrived unannounced and asked to see him. I heard later that the only reason he gave me an interview was because the attendant told him that I was young, blonde and good-looking.

I showed him some photographs of my work and after a little thought he ordered thirty paintings and fixed a date six months ahead for an exhibition. My first solo show. I was in shock. I had only a few paintings at the time and now had to paint fast to get thirty in six months.

It was Castelbarco who introduced me to Italian nobility and commissions poured in. I painted three portraits of the Marquis Sommi Picenardi. Afterwards he invited me to Turin. We went to the opera the first day. We went to bed the second. We stayed there for the third, fourth and fifth. Don't you love Italians?

That was my first Marquis. After, there was the Marquis D'Afflito - another gorgeous Italian. I painted him – twice.

Castelbarco also introduced me to Gabriele D'Annunzio who invited me to his chateau and I felt truly honoured. His reputation was as enormous as his ego and I knew I was not the first or the last woman to be invited to stay. Indeed he lives with his own harem which I found most disconcerting … but though I was flattered by his interest in me, I could not find the man attractive. There was I - a beautiful young woman - and in front of me was this ugly little old dwarf.

I had desperately wanted to paint his portrait. I thought "What a coup to painted Italy's most celebrated poet, novelist, playwright, lover"…. but he would not sit for me and I would not ….. succumb to his overtures so we parted with a great deal of frustration on both sides and, although I promised to return, I had no real desire to. A few days after I left a messenger arrived on a white horse bearing a poem to "La Donna D'Oro" and this ring. I was - how do you say - the one who got away.

Tadeusz finally rebelled. On a trip to Poland he had an affair of his own. He met her at the dentist, would you believe. He fell in love with this woman - I don't know why. I never saw the need to fall in love to enjoy a love affair. He would not return despite my tears and pleading. I went three times to Poland to bring him back, the third time I took Kizette and he gave in and came back with us.

I started a huge portrait of him. He said I only painted my lovers - no, he said I slept with everyone I painted, man or woman..... some truth. But we could find no peace between us. The fights got worse and worse and so he left for ever. I never finished the picture ... well I finished everything but one hand - his left hand - the wedding ring finger hand. I stopped painting then. We had hurled insults at each other - and I felt the incomplete man was just the right lasting image of him.
I was quite surprised that I cared so much that he left. I had my freedom now but freedom was something I had never lacked - I had always considered I had the right to freedom - as an artist.

I moved to this apartment and created with my sister's help a model home. It breaks my heart to leave it. It was designed by Mallet-Stevens - the master of modern design - art deco at its very best. Adrienne gave me the hallway of chrome and glass downstairs. The lines are simple, clean, curves - just like my pictures. I always maintain that people like my paintings because the line is clean and neat. Galleries always put my pictures in the middle of the walls as people are drawn to them because of this clean-ness, this neat-ness.

Do not judge me by this quick study of Rafaela. I normally take three weeks to finish a painting. I spend days underpainting.

Very soon people started to become collectors of my work. One such was the Baron Raoul Kuffner. He commissioned a portrait of his lover, Nana de Herrera, the Spanish dancer. I met her and thought "what an ugly woman". I could not imagine what the man could see in her in the way of beauty. In fact I used her in one of my group pictures - where I wanted someone coarse and vile looking. In the commissioned portrait I struggled.

I asked her to take off all her clothes that I might paint her in the nude and then I thought oh no my god she should put them back on again. I draped a bit of lace here and another bit there but I still could not get excited about the composition. Normally I can 'scent out' the elegance in my models but with her it was impossible.

Then I had a moment of inspiration. I said to her "How do you look when you are dancing? What expression do you have on your face?" She demonstrated to me the look of the flamenco dancer –her eyebrows came down, her nostrils flared and her lips pushed forward in a kind of provocative snarl. I had my picture. I saw quite a lot of the Baron. And soon he was taking me places instead of the dancer.

Commissions poured in. I was able to charge more and more. I was becoming quite rich from my own labours.

Once a young American made an appointment to see me and requested a portrait of his fiancée. She was on his arm and very beautiful. I agreed and offered to start right away. But he said no he was leaving for America the next day and I must come to America to do it. He would pay everything. I named my price and said I could not make the journey for another four months but he agreed. He wrote out the agreement on a piece of paper and signed it.

Later when I was telling friends about this, they were shocked at my fee and said I should have charged him much more. Living in New York was not cheap I was told. I thought about it and decided they were right.

So I wrote to the young man. Two weeks later he was back in Paris and asked me how much I thought was a proper fee for the job. I named a sum four times the previous amount and he immediately wrote out a new agreement without a murmur of complaint.

That was my first trip to America. Kizette stayed with my mother, as she often did. I wrote them lots of letters describing my grand lifestyle there. I was met off the boat with two Rolls Royces and taken to the luxurious Hotel Savoy. I was ready to start the portrait the next day but the family insisted I help the young lady choose a dress for the painting and we spent days going to all the fashionable couturiers in town. The husband - to-be was a young millionaire it transpired. His family owned the Bush terminal in New York.

I found the Americans a very strange breed - not easy to paint - far too sociable. We were never left alone. Guests would arrive in the middle of the sitting and be invited in. They wouldn't leave and they would talk - and talk and talk - how they would talk. I got used to it after a few days and I think in the end it was one of my best paintings. And look how good I have become at talking and painting.

I arranged an exhibition in Pittsburgh while I was out there and stayed on longer than the three weeks I had planned. The show went very well and I sold many paintings but then disaster struck.

I lost all the money in the Wall Street crash. But there were other commissions - so I stayed on to try and make up for my losses.

Then I met a beautiful man - very rich, very handsome. He offered to take me to his ranch in New Mexico for Christmas. I could not resist such an offer. So I wrote to my mother saying I would not be back for a while.

She was so angry when she got my letter, she burned all my hats. She took them one by one and dropped them into the incinerator of my apartment with Kizette watching all the while.

I really liked the Americans and their extravagant way of life. Hollywood and all the stars. Often people mis-took me for Greta Garbo. True. Once I was staying at Salsamaggiore in Italy and the manager came to me and said there was a crowd of people outside saying that Greta Garbo was in the hotel. "I know you are a great painter but as a favour for the good of the hotel could you possibly pretend to be Greta Garbo for a moment and go out and speak to them." I agreed to do this for him. "But what if they ask for your autograph?" he said. "I shall sign Greta Garbo" I replied and I did.

Let us have a moment of silence - reverence for Rafaela's mouth. Ah that was something to remember.

Some music starts to play.

What's this? Clothilde thinks we need more music. Ah, this is the American - Cole Porter.

Tamara sings I'VE GOT YOU UNDER MY SKIN by Cole Porter to Rafaela in the painting as she works on the mouth.

Cole Porter has been living and working near here in Paris for some time. I met him once.

I like Clothilde's choice of music. After Je l'ai tellement dans la peau - she gives us - I've got you under my skin. Same sentiment.

Back in Paris I picked up my life as before. I had the most illustrious customers for my portraits. I painted the Grand Duke Gabriel Constantinovitch Romanov, the grand-son of the Tsar's brother. I painted King Alfonso of Spain. He said I bossed him around too much during the sitting. He said "We are not accustomed to being addressed in such a manner." To which I replied

"And we are not accustomed to models who talk so much."

But we became good friends. We would take trips in his automobile into the French country. One day we had a flat tyre and while the chauffeur was fixing it, the King got talking to some passers-by. He asked them what they did for a living, trying to be very gracious, and they replied that since the local mill was closed down, they were unemployed. To which his Majesty replied "I too am unemployed!"

More and more people were becoming unemployed. The chaos was starting again. It was all beginning to come apart - again.

But my life was still intact and I fought to keep myself buoyant- even as the political world started to slide.

But I tried to vary my choice of models more and more - not just the rich and famous but ordinary people too now. Once I painted an old man. I found him at the Academie de La Grande Chaumière - a model but in rags. I took him home and said he must sit dressed exactly as he was. His face had such sadness.

One day he took from his wallet a faded cutting - it was about Rodin's sculpture The Kiss and mentioned the name of the male model for it. "That was me," he said. I could not believe it. That beautiful body was now this raggedy old man.

I was living alone now. I had sent Kizette to a boarding school in England, run by the same order of nuns as her Paris school; from there she would go to Oxford. I had my diversions and company whenever I craved it. No need of a husband really - except perhaps for complete financial security.

I had one offer from a Dr. Sergei Voronoff whom I had won over at a health spa on Lake Como. He was making a lot of money selling an anti-ageing potion made from monkey glands. He was Russian and offered me anything I wanted. He described what our life would be like together. We would travel and stay in the best of hotels. In the morning he would take me to the couturier and we would buy clothes together - then an enormous lunch - in the afternoons we would buy jewels at Cartier's or Tiffany's. In the evening I would wear everything we had bought that day and we would dine in the best restaurants in Europe. "But when would I paint?" I asked him. "Oh, there would be no need to paint." He said. "I have all the money we need." How little he understood.

Later he married an eighteen year old Russian beauty and gave her the lifestyle he described. After a couple of years of this living, she was unrecognisable - she had grown so fat from eating chocolate and lying around in bed all day. I looked at her and was glad I had escaped.

But I did succumb to my next offer. Marriage to Rollie gave me a title and he was so much wiser. He was prepared to let me keep the life I already enjoyed. And now I am Baroness Kuffner - a titled lady. We had been lovers on and off since I had painted the ugly Nana de Hererra. But when Rollie's ailing wife died, he was free to marry and proposed.

I nearly resisted him even then but it was my mother who finally persuaded me I would be mad to say no. "When will you ever get such an offer again?" And so we married and we have achieved a very happy living arrangement. We stay in separate apartments. He bought the apartment above this but more often he stays at the Westminster Hotel. But we meet for dinner at Maxim's, or elsewhere, most nights. I am expected there shortly.

We even stay in separate hotels on holiday. Last year when we went to Venice, I stayed at the Excelsior and he at the Danielli. We do not cramp each others style. He still has his big game hunting, his guns, his property. I have my painting, my friends.

We went to Egypt for our honeymoon - six years ago it was now - and then on to Hungary to his estate. His family provided the Austro-Hungarian Emperor Franz Joseph with beef and beer and received their title for services rendered. He inherited land throughout Central Europe. It was on a short break we were having in the Austrian Alps that I first heard the Hitler youth - marching by, singing. A chill ran down my spine. I could feel history repeating itself and I know now it is time to get out.

Even a few years ago, I was returning from a visit to Poland and the train stopped in Berlin in the early morning. I thought suddenly what a good idea to hop off and visit some friends for lunch and then continue my journey in the evening. Hitler had not long been in power but already the streets were filled with Nazi uniforms and the people seemed afraid. My friend was happy to see me but she was very anxious and said "How did you get a permit?"

"Permit?" I said. "What permit?" She was very upset and said "This is terrible. You must go to the police at once and tell them who you are." Well it was terrible. They were very rude and took away my passport. But they took me to their chief who was sitting there in Nazi uniform, the red band on his arm. He looked very fierce and I was really afraid.

"You are a French citizen?" he said. I said "Yes." But then he looked again at my name and says "Are you the Madame Lempicka who paints the covers of Die Dame magazine?" I said "Yes, I am." He said "My wife loves your painting and has saved all those covers. I am going to let you go now with just a small fine but you must promise never to come back."

It was frightening then but the situation now is far worse. And so I have finally persuaded Rollie to sell up and go to America - this weekend we sail for New York. He still calls it a long vacation but I am fearful we will never return. Europe is too dangerous to remain in one moment longer.

Why does this always happen to me. First in 1917 and

now in 1939. Just when things are perfect, it gets all destroyed.

And Kizette wont come with me to America - she has gone with my sister on a visit to Warsaw - at this time of all times. They are mad. I am sick with worry but she is wilful and says that America is a barbarian country. She would rather live in a civilised country at war than in a primitive one like America in peacetime. She thinks it safer. She is not making anything of her life. She travels and will not settle at her writing which I am sure she could make something of if she put her mind to it. She is lazy and over-educated.

She throws down her brushes in a temper.

I must stop now. I am tired of talking. I will get Clothilde to show you out.. Clothilde. Clothilde.

I am sure you have enough for your little interview. I have told you much more than you would ever get had you asked questions.

And at least we have been able to bring Rafaela to life ....my beauty........

The music of MON AMI by Kurt Weill is heard.

What's this? More music! Chlotilde I wanted you to come. Oh, this is Kurt Weill. He has already fled to America. Now we must follow.

She sings along to the record while she removes her overall.

My Madelon of Paris
She'll laugh and dance and sing
To cheer the weary soldier
At his homecoming
A little room together
An hour of love to spend
Comme ça, you arm around me
O mon ami, my friend

But she, ah, she remembers
That other love and joy
The first, the best, the dearest
Tired soldier boy
A narrow room alone now
Rain on the roof above
And he will sleep forever.
O mon ami, my love

My Madelon of Paris
She does not sit and grieve
But sings away her sorrow
To cheer the soldier's leave
For life is short and funny
And love must have an end
An hour may be forever
O mon ami, my friend

On the closing notes of the song Tamara kisses her fingers and lays the kiss on Rafaela's lips.

She turns to the audience, dismissive again.

Enough!

She leaves the stage.

WHAT HAPPENED NEXT...

With her husband, Baron Raoul Kuffner, Tamara left for America as planned in 1939. After a brief stay in New York they settled in Beverley Hills in Los Angeles and mixed with Hollywood society during the war years.

Her daughter Kizette joined them in 1941. Tamara's artistic output declined. Kizette married a Texan geologist, Harold Foxhall and they had two daughters. In 1943 the Kuffners moved to New York and Tamara experimented with Abstract Art and began to work with a spatula. Her works were not popular and did not sell.

In 1960 the Baron died and Tamara was deeply affected. She moved to Houston, Texas to be near Kizette who started to manage her mother's affairs. In 1973 a major retrospective of Tamara's work in Paris brought about a renewal of interest in her work, i.e. the paintings of her Paris years. Prices have continued to rise for these works and her pictures have been known to change hands for $1,000,000. Jack Nicholson, Barbra Streisand and Madonna have been collectors of her work.

In 1974 she moved to Cuernavaca in Mexico and when she fell seriously ill in 1979, Kizette moved in to nurse her. She died in her sleep in 1980 and, according to her mother's wishes, Kizette scattered Tamara's ashes over the crater of Mt. Popocatepetl.

** STOP PRESS **

Recent research by Laura Claridge, author of the new biography of Tamara, published in 1999, uncovered a few inexactitudes in Tamara's story. All her life Tamara was not completely truthful about her early years. It transpires that she was not born in Poland but was in fact born in Moscow of a Russian Jewish father and Polish mother. Extraordinarily wealthy, the family spent part of the year in Poland. Other details she embroidered on were her birth date, marriage and pregnancy.

BIBLIOGRAPHY

PASSION BY DESIGN, The Art and Times of Tamara de Lempicka *by Baroness Kizette de Lempicka-Foxhall as told to Charles Phillips. New York: Abbeville Press; Oxford: Phaidon, 1987.*

TAMARA DE LEMPICKA, Paris 1920-1938 *by Gioia Mori. Paris: Herscher, 1993.*

LEMPICKA *by Gilles Neret. Translated by Michael Scuffil. Khöln: Benedikt Taschen. 1993*

TAMARA DE LEMPICKA, Elegant transgressions *edited by Maurizio Calvesi and Alessandro Borghese, Catalogue for The Montreal Museum of Fine Arts, October 1994*

TAMARA DE LEMPICKA, A Life of Deco and Decadence *by Laura Claridge. New York, 1999.*